DATE DUE

In the Spotlight

Gal Gadot

by Kaitlyn Duling

Ideas for Parents and Teachers

Bullfrog Books let children practice reading informational text at the earliest reading levels. Repetition, familiar words, and photo labels support early readers.

Before Reading

• Discuss the cover photo. What does it tell them?

• Look at the picture glossary together. Read and discuss the words.

Read the Book

• "Walk" through the book and look at the photos. Let the child ask questions. Point out the photo labels.

• Read the book to the child, or have him or her read independently.

After Reading

• Prompt the child to think more. Ask: What did you know about Gal Gadot before reading this book? What more would you like to learn about her after reading it?

Bullfrog Books are published by Jump!
5357 Penn Avenue South
Minneapolis, MN 55419
www.jumplibrary.com

Library of Congress Cataloging-in-Publication Data

Names: Duling, Kaitlyn, author.
Title: Gal Gadot / by Kaitlyn Duling.
Description: Minneapolis, MN : Jump!, Inc., [2019]
Series: In the spotlight | Bullfrog Books.
For ages 5–8, grade levels K–3rd grade.
Includes index.
Identifiers: LCCN 2018017592 (print)
LCCN 2018019228 (ebook)
ISBN 9781641281973 (ebook)
ISBN 9781641281959 (hardcover : alk. paper)
ISBN 9781641281966 (pbk.)
Subjects: LCSH: Gadot, Gal, 1985—Juvenile literature.
Actresses—United States—Biography
Juvenile literature.
Classification: LCC PN2287.G335 (ebook)
LCC PN2287.G335 D85 2018 (print)
DDC 791.4302/8092 [B]—dc23
LC record available at https://lccn.loc.gov/2018017592

Editors: Susanne Bushman & Kristine Spanier
Designer: Molly Ballanger

Photo Credits: s_bukley/Shutterstock, cover; Dia Dipasupil/Getty, 1; Jaguarps/Dreamstime, 3; Tinseltown/Shutterstock, 4, 23tl; Juanmonio/iStock, 5, 23br; Israel Sun/Rex, 6, 22bl; Martin Bernetti/Getty, 6–7; AF archive/Alamy, 8; Jeffrey Mayer/Getty, 9; monkeybusinessimages/iStock, 10–11 (family); Collection Christophel/Alamy, 10–11 (movie still), 15, 23br; Moviestore collection Ltd/Alamy, 12–13; Moviestore/Rex, 14; Nordic Photos, 16–17; Mike Coppola/Getty, 18–19; Eric Charbonneau/Rex, 20–21, 23tr; Picsfive/Shutterstock, 22t; Album/Alamy, 22br; Featureflash Photo Agency/Shutterstock, 24.

Printed in the United States of America at Corporate Graphics in North Mankato, Minnesota.

Table of Contents

Gal

This is Gal Gadot.

She is famous.

Why? She acts.

Where is Gal from?

Israel.

It is far away.

She was in contests.
She won one.
Look! A crown.
Nice!

crown

She moved.
Where? America.
She started to act.

In what? Movies.

She plays Wonder Woman.
Cool!

Wonder Woman is strong.

She fights.

She keeps people safe.

She fights with others.
Like who? Batman. Flash.

She does stunts.
Wow!

Gal helps.
She raises money.
For what?
Schools. Nice!

Gal speaks up.

We look up to her.

fans